The BTG Book of

ROCKING HORSES

ISBN 0-9545388-3-8

Designed & Published by
The Rocking Horse Shop Ltd, Fangfoss, York, YO41 5JH, England.

Old Rocking Horses

The oldest surviving rocking horse in the world is thought to have been made in the very early 1600s. It is reputed to have been ridden by the boy, born in 1600, who later became King Charles 1.

Although there appears to be no hard evidence to support the royal connection, the timber has been expertly dated to the early 1600s &, with rockers made from arcs of solid timber & a carved head & neck, the horse is typical of the very earliest style of rocking horse. The rockers, the cross pieces that separate them, & the head and neck, are made of pine. The body is solid elm with two grooves running across which may once have housed boards at the front & back of the saddle, providing a more secure seat for the rider.

On the head there is evidence of some quite detailed carving around the eyes, & nails where a horsehair mane was once fitted. It is a little over 44inches (1125mm) long overall, very heavy, & very simply made, the parts are just nailed & glued together. Though extremely battered & worn, the horse has the most wonderful patina that only comes with great age and use.

Other Rocking Horses survive from the 17th Century but only a very few. All children's toys get battered & worn in normal use, & when children grow out of them may be passed on to poorer relations until eventually they wear out & are discarded. It is therefore remarkable that any survive at all.

Before motor transport when, apart from walking, horses supplied the only decent means of travel, they were a means of teaching children how to ride. As well as being playthings then, Rocking Horses had an educational role.

Some early Rocking Horses had steep bow rockers & a fast & jerky rocking action, perhaps quite deliberately. No overweening Health & Safety considerations in those days! When a child was thrown off, he would be told to stop crying, get straight back on, and learn to ride properly, with correct balance, as on a real horse.

There may also have been an educational value in teaching children about horse harness, but this was limited since the majority of Rocking Horses have always had fixed bridles & saddles, secured in position with dome headed & wire nails. It is doubtful if there was any safety consideration in this; more likely economic.

The world's oldest rocker ? (above & right).
Relatively modern plywood version of the slab sided
horse: (opposite) & (below right) with printed flower
design, made by Anthony Dew, & flat pack version
(below) designed by Swiss engineer
Rudolf Wurgler with hand
painted patterns.

'Proper' Rocking Horses

    Fully carved Rocking Horses soon came to be made with four separate legs jointed into the body, the carving more naturalistic & horse-like. As the craft progressed a distinctive Rocking Horse look developed, which gradually became a tradition. 'Proper' Rocking Horses have a number of essential characteristics & even today, makers who depart from the traditional aesthetic are likely to encounter resistance: "Well it certainly looks very nice, but I must say I prefer the real thing". Perhaps this is just a natural resistance to change. Nevertheless the traditional form of the Rocking Horse has come to have a special & lasting place in the affections of the public at large, especially the British.

    The bodies of 'proper' traditional Rocking Horses are slender (in contrast to real horses), the form simplified or stylised. Legs are stretched

4

out four square front and rear & bolted or clench nailed at each hoof to thin timber bow shaped rockers. The ends of bows are shaped to form stops to prevent the horse from overturning. Manes & tails are real hair, either horsehair or from cow tails which has an attractive natural curl. Bridles, saddles & straps are of brown leather, with coloured saddlecloths edged with decorative braid, & usually nailed on, secured with dome & fancy brass nails.

Paintwork is typically dapple grey, usually stippled in black over a white or blue/grey basecoat. Eyes are glass, set in carved recesses & rimmed with red paint. Eyelashes are black, sometimes very delicately painted. The insides of the ears, nostrils & mouth are painted red, with individual teeth picked out in white.

Natural wood finishes, stained &/or lacquered, are a relatively modern phenomenon: contemporary eyes considering it a pity to cover all that wood & woodcarving with layers of paint. Some modern makers also use different natural timbers & finishes to good effect.

Horses were generally carved of yellow pine, a straight grained softwood into which a skilled craftsman could carve great detail, expression & character. There are upwards of twenty blocks of solid timber in a horse, glued together & carved. The body is hollow. In production workshops horses would be blocked up & rough carved in the Spring, stacked to dry out through the Summer, & brought down for finishing ready for delivery to the shops in the Autumn, Christmas being the big deadline for all toymakers.

Legs were made in beech for its greater strength, bow rockers in ash or beech. Stands were often pine, with turned beech posts. But many other timbers have been used. It is said that in the latter half of the 19th Century as iron ships replaced wooden ones & their skills ceased to be needed, many ship carvers (of figureheads & so on) turned to making carousel horses & Rocking Horses.

The best of the late Victorian Rocking Horses combine excellent craftsmanship & an artist's eye, informed by a good knowledge of real horses, & are very beautiful, as well as practical playthings.

(opposite page) A particularly fine example of a late 19th Century Rocking Horse made by F. H. Ayres & Co. Unrestored & in completely original condition, such horses are now very sought after, & expensive!

(right) The busy production workshop of Barker & Sons Ltd of Birmingham, taken in about 1927.

The Best of Times

The heyday of the traditional Rocking Horse, as we now know it, was between 1880 & the 1930s, when many thousands were made & it became the 'must have' toy for every nursery. Factory production methods were on the rise & the bigger manufacturers employed copy carving machines to speed the rough carving process & increase productivity. Smaller production workshops relied on the work of hand carvers, avoiding the need for costly & specialised machinery but sometimes at the expense of consistency of product (which of course may not be a bad thing in craft work), or quality (which is).

Makers were also actively developing designs for new rocking mechanisms. These were partly intended to improve on the 'conventional bow rocker & overcome objections to it, such as its "liability to breakage & to rock over & injure the rider & pinch the feet of lookers on, while it either wears the floor cover or if there is none is apt to be noisy" - a rather damning critique of bow rockers quoted from an 1887 patent application by G. & J. Lines for an improved mounting for Rocking Horses.

One idea involved "a peculiar form of spring", an india rubber thong & a vibrating beam in a "device whereby two or more children may ride at the same

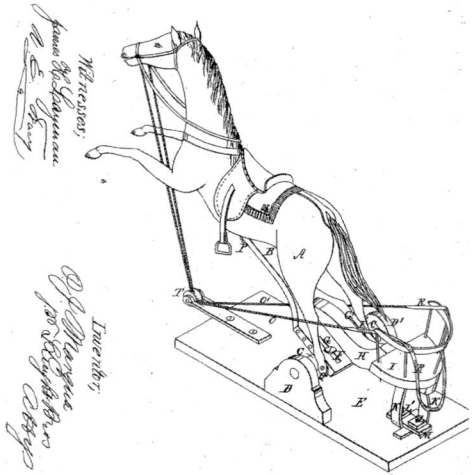

The patent application drawing (above) for Philip Marqua's 1865 'improved' rocking device, & (below) the one that really did the business, Marqua's 1878 US patent, filed in Britain on 29th January 1880.

P. MARQUA.
Hobby-Horse.

No. 208,531.   Patented Oct. 1, 1878.

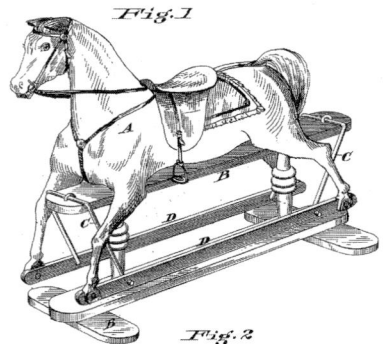

6

time" in a patent filed by one Philip J. Marqua of Cincinatti in the USA back in 1865. Most of the many ingenious designs for improving on the traditional bow shaped rocker, using levers, coil or leaf springs were, like Marqua's 1865 effort, too complicated or impractical to be viable, but a few were produced commercially & have now become very collectable. Marqua himself went on to develop & patent what became by far the most successful & widely used design.

Marqua's idea, as is the way with the best ideas, was simple, practical, & it worked beautifully. It employed what have become known as 'swing irons', mounted on a stand resting on the floor, sometimes referred as the 'safety stand'. It gives a very effective rocking action, does not 'travel', requires much less space than bows and is, arguably, safer. The key thing is that "... the bars (ie swing irons) are so hung ... as to bring the lower ends ... closer together than at the top, for the purpose of producing a swinging rocking motion similar to a canter". When the horse rocks forward the back rises, & when the horse rocks back the head rises.

This gives the horse its distinctive rocking action (rather different from that experienced on a bows mounted horse) & also incorporates an effective stop, in that the horse can rock only so far & then stops & rocks back. In Marqua's patent a significant additional benefit was, he says, the ease with which the stand can be "taken apart for convenience in packing for shipment". Marqua's patent was filed in 1878 in the USA & in Britain just over a year later.

They're off! A fine line-up at a Southport, Lancashire day nursery in the 1920s.

Lines 'Jubilee Safety Hobby Horse', so named - in a Gamages toyshop advertisement - because it was introduced in 1887, Queen Victoria's Jubilee year.

In 1887 George & Joseph Lines filed a patent application in London for an "invention relating to certain improvements connected with rocking horses". The horse's belly was secured to an arc of timber, in turn attached to "an oscillating device", the whole thing mounted on a four legged stand. In making their case, the brothers objected to bow rockers "as usually constructed" (quoted on page 6), & criticise "swinging bars ... mounted on a stand" (presumably a reference to Marqua's device) as 'cumbrous &

expensive to manufacture & does not produce the required cantering motion". In fact, Lines 'invention' appears to be little more than a variant of Marqua's idea with the swing irons upside down. It is equally effective in use, but in fact was probably more 'cumbrous' & expensive to manufacture. Interestingly, Lines Jubilee type Rocking Horse seems to have caught on in the USA, whilst Marqua type swing iron stands became much the most popular type to be made in Britain, not least by Lines themselves.

Identifying & Buying an Old Horse

Old rocking horses, or ones that look old, may be found for sale at auctions or car boot sales, in antique shops or newspaper advertisements, or on the internet. Rocking Horses of most interest to collectors, & for which the highest prices are paid, will be professionally made by one of the top makers (rarer models are particularly sought after), typically late Victorian or early 20th Century, & preferably with all or most of the original paintwork & saddlery intact.

Some have maker's marks or plates which makes identification easy, but if not they may still be identified by

such features as the style of stand post employed, the style & idiosyncrasies of the carving, paintwork, metalwork &/or other distinguishing features. Sometimes name plates or stencils with names such as Selfridges, Gamages, Harrods or others are found on the stand - this is the name of the toyshop from which the horse was originally bought, rather than a maker's name.

In its heyday Tri-ang Toys, the company which grew out of Lines Bros, was probably the world's biggest manufacturer of children's toys of all descriptions, with an incredibly extensive range.

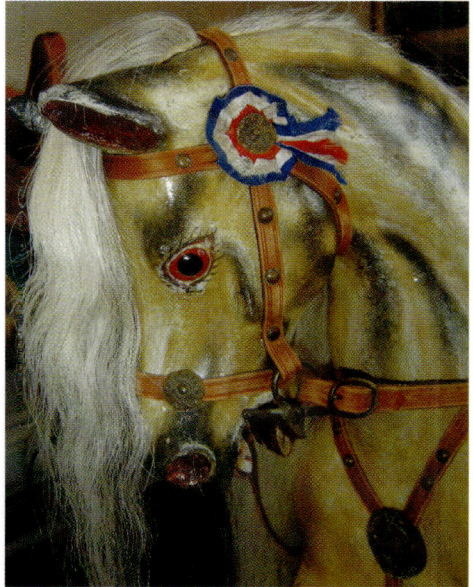

Brass chest insignia of Lines Jubilee Horse (top left) & close-up of head (above). This horse has been professionally restored by an expert - a fine animal!

Stevenson Bros present one of their new reproduction horses to Queen Elizabeth in her Jubilee year, 2002.

" SPORTIBOY " SAFETY ROCKING HORSES 3002
Beautifully painted and dappled by experts. Constructed from
well-seasoned timber. Saddles are detachable. Nicely varnished
stand. Six sizes.

Model			1	2	3	4	5	6
Overall Length	...		36″	44″	52″	57″	64″	70″

Tri-ang donkey, plastic moulding, tubular steel rocker.

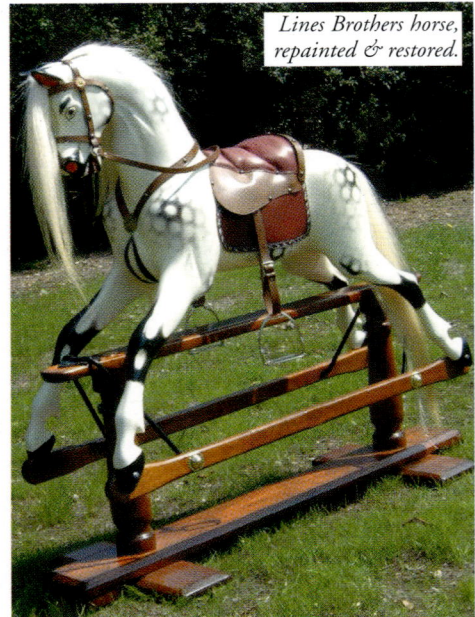

Lines Brothers horse, repainted & restored.

Tri-ang Sportiboy, in un-restored original condition.

When Lines Bros, or Tri-ang Toys as it was from around 1927, made Rocking Horses they made dozens of types, styles & sizes ranging from simple little horses for toddlers, to large & magnificent 'extra carved' steeds, & just about every possible variation in between. The 1937/8 catalogue contains a simple stool horse, several 'hollow' horses, a couple of Mickey Mouse rockers, a tubular metal rocker with a simple wooden head & their fully carved traditional 'Sportiboy Safety Rocking Horses' with detachable saddles, in six sizes. By that time many of the more expensive top end horses were no longer being produced, but the catalogue still lists 32 different rocking & push along toys.

10

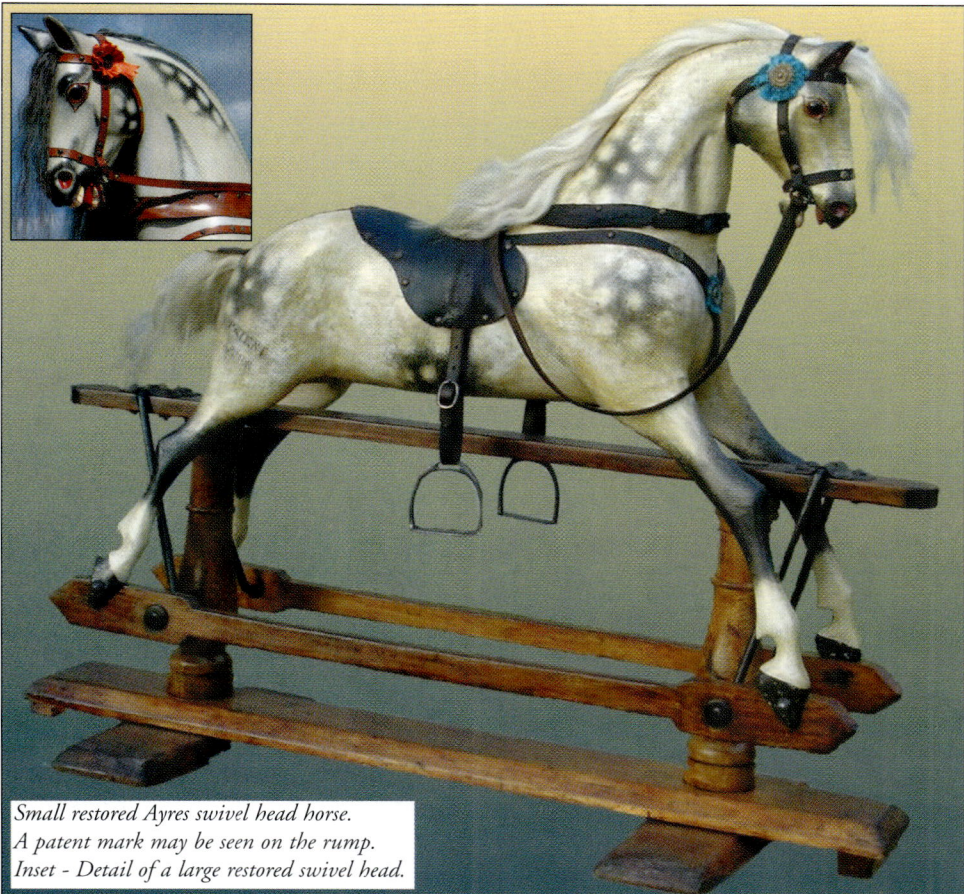

Small restored Ayres swivel head horse.
A patent mark may be seen on the rump.
Inset - Detail of a large restored swivel head.

F. H. Ayres were manufacturers of sporting goods - billiard tables, croquet & cricket equipment etc. It seems that in everything they made they strived for top quality. The best of Ayres Rocking Horses are generally regarded as the best of them all - beautifully made & finished by craftspeople who really knew what a good rocking horse should be like - the epitome of the craft. Quality Rocking Horses often have heads which are angled to look off to one side or the other, giving them a bit of 'life' otherwise lacking. Ayres better, 'extra carved' horses had this feature, as did some other makers, but Frederick Ayres developed an interesting variant: in 1886 he filed a patent for a Rocking Horse on which the head was made to swivel to the left or right, 'steered' by the reins. An interesting novelty & few were made, so surviving swivel head horses are rare & valuable.

Collinson Rocking Horse - this one has been completely restored: the boldly painted dappling & teeth, the blonde hair, the nails for eyes & the red corduroy saddle seat are among typical Collinson features.

Queen Victoria is said to have admired the dapple grey when she visited Collinson's factory in Smithdown Rd, Liverpool, & after that the dapple grey became their standard horse, produced in at least 6 sizes. They also made versions covered in brown or black fur fabric, with the same woodwork underneath. Stands are generally the first thing to look at when starting to indentify the maker of a particular horse. Collinson stands, usually parana pine, have rectangular tapered posts, with two hardboard diamond shapes pinned on the top rail above each post, which conceal the heads of the nails used to fix the stand together.

Collinson horses are painted in a bold style, some would say crude, with lots of dark dappling, distinctive black eyelashes & bright red nostrils, ears & mouth. Often the mane & tail is blonde cow tail hair, the saddle seat red corduroy, the leather brown. On later models the nailed on bridle & strapping may be plastic or leathercloth.

The carving tends to be fairly basic, the construction simple, just glue & nails. The horse, including the legs, is usually made of pine or other softwood, & occasionally even chipboard or plywood was used in places.

Leeway, in original condition.

Collinson horse in original condition.

Leeway (the trademark for Patterson Edwards), Baby Carriages Ltd (BCL - related to Collinson's), Swallow (G. Woodrow & Co), Barkers, & one or two other makers are also readily identifiable, once you know what to look for. But with some makers, eg Paul Leach, J.R. & T. Smith, Wilson or Ajoy, identification can be problematic. There are a number of reasons for this.

Some larger makers, notably Lines, supplied fittings to other makers. Thus Lines brackets appear on several other makes of horse. Also, carvers could transfer their skills & style to another company, or set up on their own. Makers may copy features - eg they may

13

   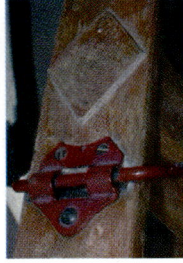 

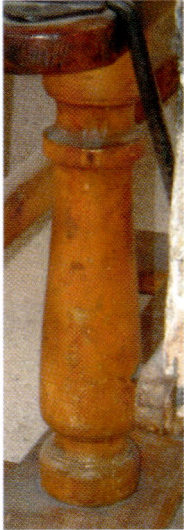    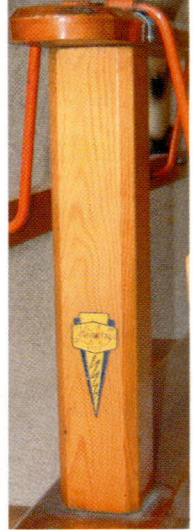

| *Lines* | *Tri-ang* | *Ayres* | *Collinson* | *Leeway* |

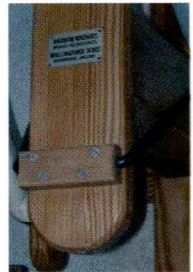

Advertisement from Gamages toyshop 1932 catalogue.

GAMAGES' SAFETY ROCKING HORSE

Very strongly made and finished in best style. Quite safe and practically unbreakable.

No.			Length of Stand	Height to Saddle			Price £ s. d.
1	..	..	36 ins. ..	29½ ins. ..	..	..	2 5 0
2	..	..	44 ,, ..	33 ,, ..	..	..	3 3 6
3	..	..	52 ,, ..	37 ,, ..	..	..	4 7 6
4	..	..	57½ ,, ..	39½ ,, ..	..	..	5 7 6

Also in Superior Quality. Stand 44 ins. Saddle 33 ins. Price £4 10 0
With all plated fittings. £9 0 0

Haddon Rockers, (right) stands have simple plywood brackets & maker's plate.

(Below) Stencil on base of an Ayres stand shows the patent date, not date of manufacture.

14

Lines Bros horses often have maker's marks such as the thistle emblem (left) often in pressed brass, sometimes without the lettering, or the Tri-ang mark (right) used after about 1927, often as a transfer.

reproduce Ayres design features or posts (if you're going to emulate somebody, choose the best!). The old makers almost never signed their work: contemporary makers almost always do, so the correct identification of early makers continues to be the subject of much discussion among restorers & enthusiasts.

Increasingly, 'fakes' are appearing on the market. Some are cleverly distressed, easily mistaken for old horses when they are not. Of course no reputable rocking horse person would do this, but sometimes sellers mislead buyers & it can be disappointing to find that the lovely '100 year old' English Rocking Horse you bought at such a bargain price was actually made last year in Indonesia.

Be clear about what you want to buy, & why. There is little point in spending a lot of money on a beautiful museum piece if all you want is an everyday horse for the children to ride.

Similarly, it would be a pity to waste your money on a horse which may then need a lot more spending on it just to make it usable, & of course, safe for children to use.

Think carefully & seek professional advice, especially before you start to strip tack & paint off your old horse. It is all too easy to destroy value & interest which is impossible to replace.

Fine restored mid-19th Century horse, maker's name unknown.

Cheap import.

15

Some makers produced 'affordable' horses - simple plank or box bodies & minimal carving, but retaining some of the elements of a 'proper' Rocking Horse.

Decline

Making a traditional fully carved Rocking Horse was, & is, a highly skilled & labour intensive craft involving a wide variety of skills. Only limited mechanisation is possible or practicable if the traditional Rocking Horse shape & look is not to be subverted. The recession of the late 1920s hit many small manufacturers, especially those like Rocking Horse makers whose products were non-essential. Many more closed during the Second World War, never to re-start.

The post war years saw a continuing decline in craftsman made toys, & the growth of mass produced toys, usually imported & often shoddy. It was a reaction to this that lead to the formation of the British Toymaker's Guild in 1956.

Collinsons were virtually the only maker of any size to keep going.

Remarkably, five generations of Collinsons had made their distinctive dapple greys when they finally gave up the unequal struggle in the early 1990s. Apart from Collinsons, by the late 1960s only a few very small traditional makers survived, including James Bosworthick in Suffolk & Andrew Booth in Devon, & they were getting older. Rocking Horse making seemed set to die out, like so many other traditional crafts.

Revival

Margaret Spencer always liked Rocking Horses & made her first one in 1966, when she was then in her early 40s. Inspired by her father Andrew Booth, though largely self taught, she eventually took over from him, working from her Somerset home. Describing herself as 'Rocking Horse Specialist', as well as making & restoring Margaret wrote two books on how to make Rocking Horses.

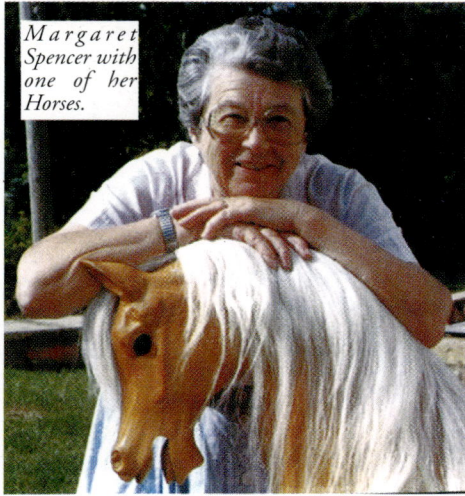

Margaret Spencer with one of her Horses.

She eventually retired in 1996 but Margaret Spencer Rocking Horses still trades, under new owners in Essex.

Art school graduates Stuart & Pam MacPherson became interested in making Rocking Horses in the early 1970s, partly because daughter Anwen was obsessed with one & refused to play with anything else. Stuart gave up teaching in the belief that he could make a living making Rocking Horses. He calls this his 'worst mistake', but is joking (probably). Based in rural North Wales, he & Pam have made Rocking Horses their life's career, & are a great partnership.

As well as restoration work & making new horses in the traditional manner, APES, as their company is named (after the initial letters of their family's first names), have designed & made fibreglass Rocking Horses based on real horse breeds in lifelike poses. Pam & Stuart are staunch defenders of traditional bow rockers, preferring them to the ubiquitous swing iron stand.

One of a series of horses made by the MacPherson's based on real pony breeds.

17

Rocking Horse maker James Bosworthick was nearing retirement when Anthony Dew first visited him in his Suffolk workshop in 1976. Ex seafarer, joiner & woodwork teacher, Dew had already carved a Rocking Horse as part of a college project. Encouraged by the old man, he returned to his Yorkshire workshop intent on starting his own

Anthony Dew at work (top right), & two of his horses (top left & below).

rocking horse making business.

His ambition was to make the best carved Rocking Horses he could: his own, but in the traditional hand carved manner. He persevered, his Rocking Horses started to sell, & in 1984 he gave up the 'day job', moved to a new workshop & took on his first employee. Rocking Horses had taken over his life completely. He wrote 'Making Rocking Horses', a how-to-do-it book on making & restoration, the first book devoted to the subject.

Anthony Dew & Company went on to become the leading supplier of plans & accessories for Rocking Horse makers & restorers, as well as continuing to develop & make new hand carved horses, mostly to individual commission, & the restoration of battered old ones.

18

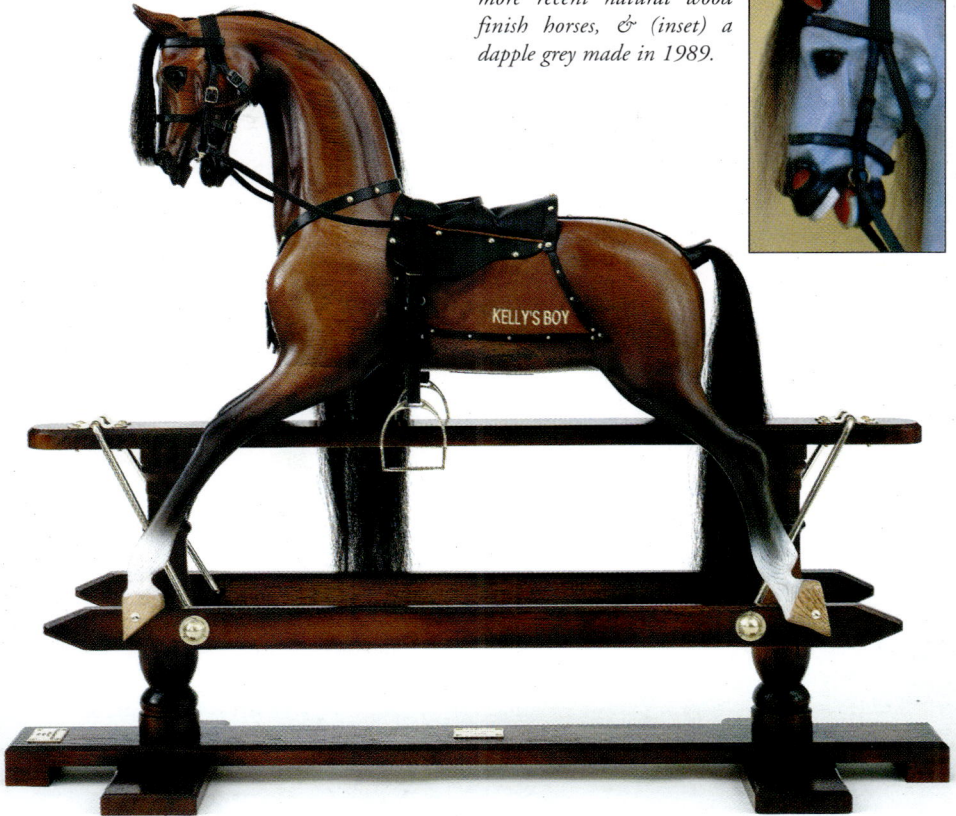

Inspired by their Uncle James (the same James Bosworthick mentioned above) Tony & Marc Stevenson formed a partnership in 1982. Tony served & paid for an apprenticeship in the craft, the intention being to make the finest Rocking Horses & 'improve the quality of children's lives'.

At that time old Rocking Horses were very undervalued & often sold for tiny sums, or were simply discarded. In that climate it was difficult for any aspiring maker to charge a price high enough to make any sort of living from the craft, let alone a good one. It was perhaps the Stevenson's achievement to put into their Rocking Horses what was then an unusually high quality of craftsmanship, & also, by dint of extremely good marketing (not something craft toymakers are usually very good at) to sell them for what were then seen as exceptionally high prices.

19

Other makers would seek to emulate the quality of Stevenson Brothers work & their prices, but rarely with equivalent success. In 2006 they were said to be 'making around 400 Rocking Horses a year with a team of 18 craftsmen'. By the standards of most craft toymakers that is big business.

Tin & Skin & other Materials

Pressed metal 'Mobo' Horses , made by D. Sebel & Co, will arouse happy childhood memories in many people of a certain age. The basic horse was produced with a variety of painted finishes & mountings, including one with wheels at each hoof which 'walked' when the footrests were pressed.

Some Rocking Horses, many made in Germany between the wars, had wooden frames & were stuffed with wood wool with a hessian covering onto which was stitched skin. The skin of a foal or calf was used: more a job for a taxidermist than a toymaker! Modern versions are stuffed with more up-to-date materials & covered with artificial fur fabrics.

Skin or fabric covered horses are mostly small & light, & many are made with their hooves fixed to a solid wooden platform with wheels, in turn secured with bolts & wing nuts to bow rockers. It can then be either a Rocking Horse or push-along toy at will: a convertible!

Metal Mobo horses. On a stand with springs, on bow rockers, & (below) a pair of 'walking' horses, Mobo on the left, on the right a modern plastic copy, made in India.

Skin coloured convertible horse

20

Well used
Medium size
Haddon horse.

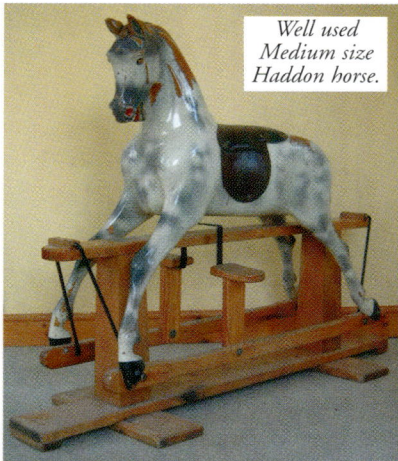

Judy Fergusson
& her horses.

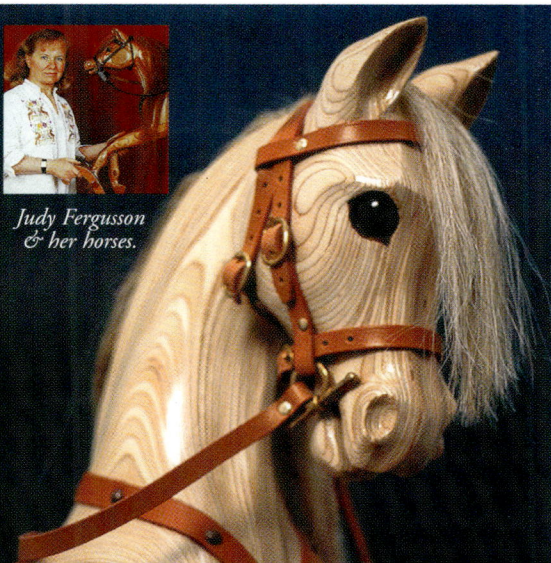

Ian Armstrong
laminated horse.

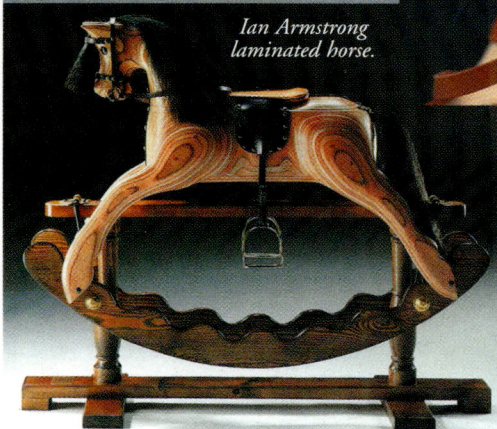

Another 'Judy F'
design.

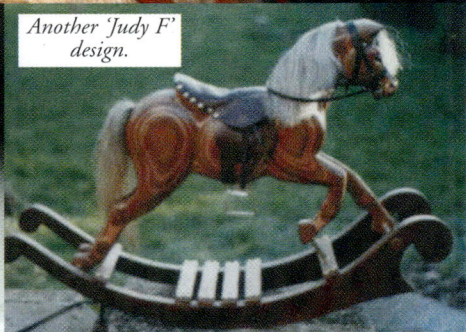

In the mid 1970s, Haddon Rocking Horses started to produce glass fibre Rocking Horses using traditional wooden horses as the models for their mouldings. Though lacking the feel of wood, fibreglass is relatively light weight & hard wearing. Some time in the 80s Haddons took over Relko, a maker of laminated horses & is still in business, under new ownership, producing Rocking Horses in glass fibre, plywood & 'composite materials'.

Other plywood laminate designs were successfully developed by Judy Fergusson, whose company, 'Judy F Designs', is based at Small Horse Farm on the Isle of Wight (she clearly has a thing about little horses as she also keeps Shetland ponies), & Ian Armstrong in Durham. Laminated horses are strong, resistant to temperature & humidity changes, & have a striking appearance with swirling patterns.

21

Flannagans.

On the other hand, Flannagans Horses with their appealing & robust construction, were definitely for children. Flannagans horses were carved (alas no longer) by Kevin Bonner in several timber finishes as well as laminated, & featured a running rabbit on the stand.

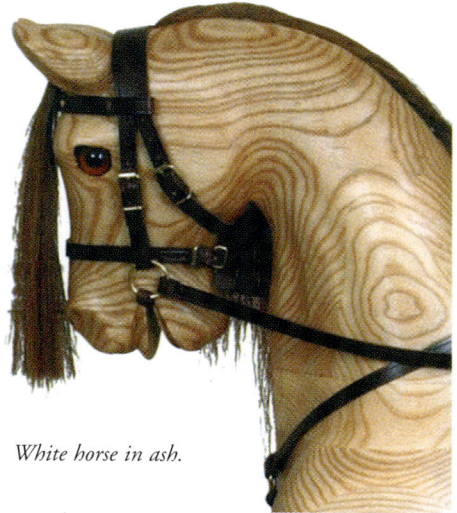
White horse in ash.

Revival continued

From the 1980s to the present, many new Rocking Horse makers & restorers have started in business, mostly a single craftsperson or partnership, the small scale allowing an individual approach to their craft & a personal interest in their customers. The best have high levels of skill & knowledge & I regret this book is too small to mention all but a few.

Trevor Wiffen produced very individualistic carvings with natural wood finishes, beautiful & naturalistic horses in active poses, as if prancing, sometimes with other animals or birds carved into the design. They are Rocking Horses, but as much decorative sculptural pieces as everyday playthings for children.

A Wiffen horse.

Though the style of their Rocking Horses is more conventional than the two above, White Horses have made them in various natural timbers - ash, oak, walnut & mahogany - as well as the ubiquitous dapple grey. Terry White recalls his early struggles: on one occasion he blocked up three horses in a hurry only to find he'd glued the heads on the wrong end! However, after making many hundreds of horses over the past twenty years, he reckons by now he has just about got the hang of it!

22

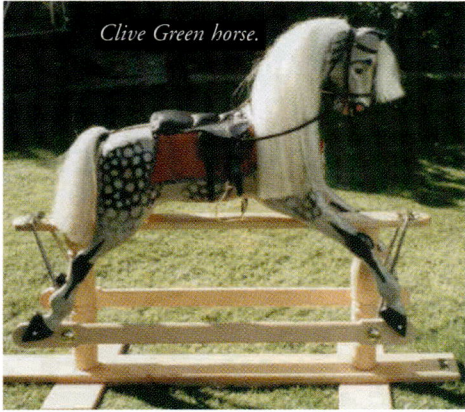
Clive Green horse.

Clive Green, a past Chairman of the British Toymaker's Guild, is co-author of the only book on 'Restoring Rocking Horses'. Mention must also be made of Australian restorer & enthusiast Patricia Mullins, whose 'The Rocking Horse, A History of Moving Toy Horses' was published in 1992. This superb book remains the standard reference work on the subject. (Both books regrettably are currently out of print).

An early Lines
(or possibly Wilson!)
nursery rocker,
with paintwork in superb
original condition.

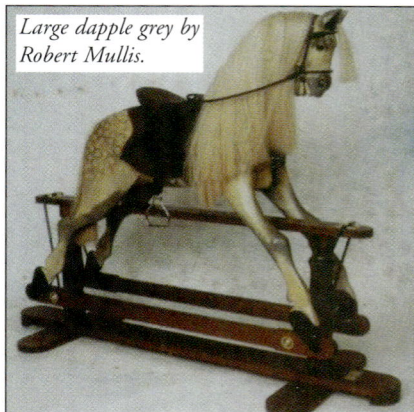

Large dapple grey by Robert Mullis.

Robert Mullis, Anthony Jackson, the Tildesleys & Sam Glass are also makers & restorers with a wealth of experience. Glass once worked for Anthony Dew & Co but is now self employed & calls himself as a 'jobbing Rocking Horse maker', a rare profession!

Several former Stevenson Bros craftspeople run Rocking Horse making & restoration businesses of their own. Alex Kinane, trading under the

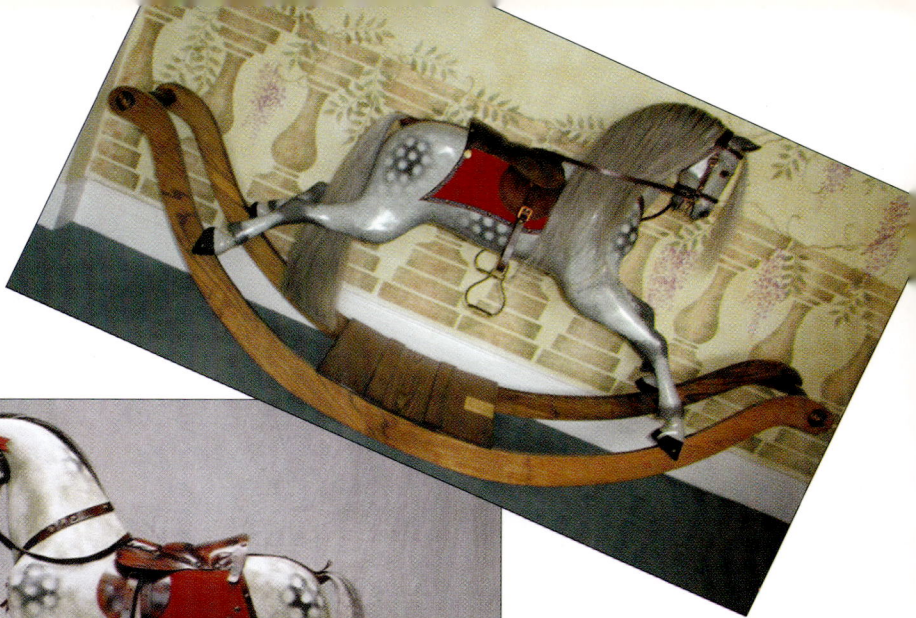

Rocking Horse made by the Tildesley's (above) who trade as Classic Rocking Horses.

One of Anthony Jackson's new horses (left) with 'antique' traditional grey paintwork, &, the man himself (opposite page) in his workshop.

name Legends, is a fine craftsman who has made reproduction Rocking Horses virtually indistinguishable from the originals, even to a trained eye. Also David & Noreen Kiss, who worked with Stevensons in their early days & now run 'Rocking Horse Workshop' in Shropshire.

Among more recent notable converts to the craft, concerning themselves with high quality restoration work, collecting & dealing, as well as the detective work of identity spotting, are Jane Hooker, Jan Rusling & Debbie Walsh.

In the early days of the revival even 'experts' knew little, & horses were frequently wrongly attributed. Though this does still happen, thanks to the exchange of information among people such as these, our knowledge base has grown enormously, & keeps growing.

Alongside the growth in recent years of new small businesses making & restoring Rocking Horses, lifestyle magazines & several TV programmes have encouraged a wider general interest in antique Rocking Horses as valuable artifacts. Perhaps because of their size, in the past Rocking Horses were never collected in the way that, for example, dolls or teddy bears have been. They were neglected & under-priced, but no longer.

A growing number of enthusiasts, collectors & dealers are recognising the beauty & value of old Rocking Horses: top quality examples are becoming harder to find & prices are going up. But bargains can still be found & you need not pay the earth for a good, well made traditional wooden Rocking Horse, perhaps in need of some tlc.

Swing irons on plate spring stand (above) - an Ayres 1895 patent. Fine horse, fully restored by Jan Rusling, & (inset) before she started.

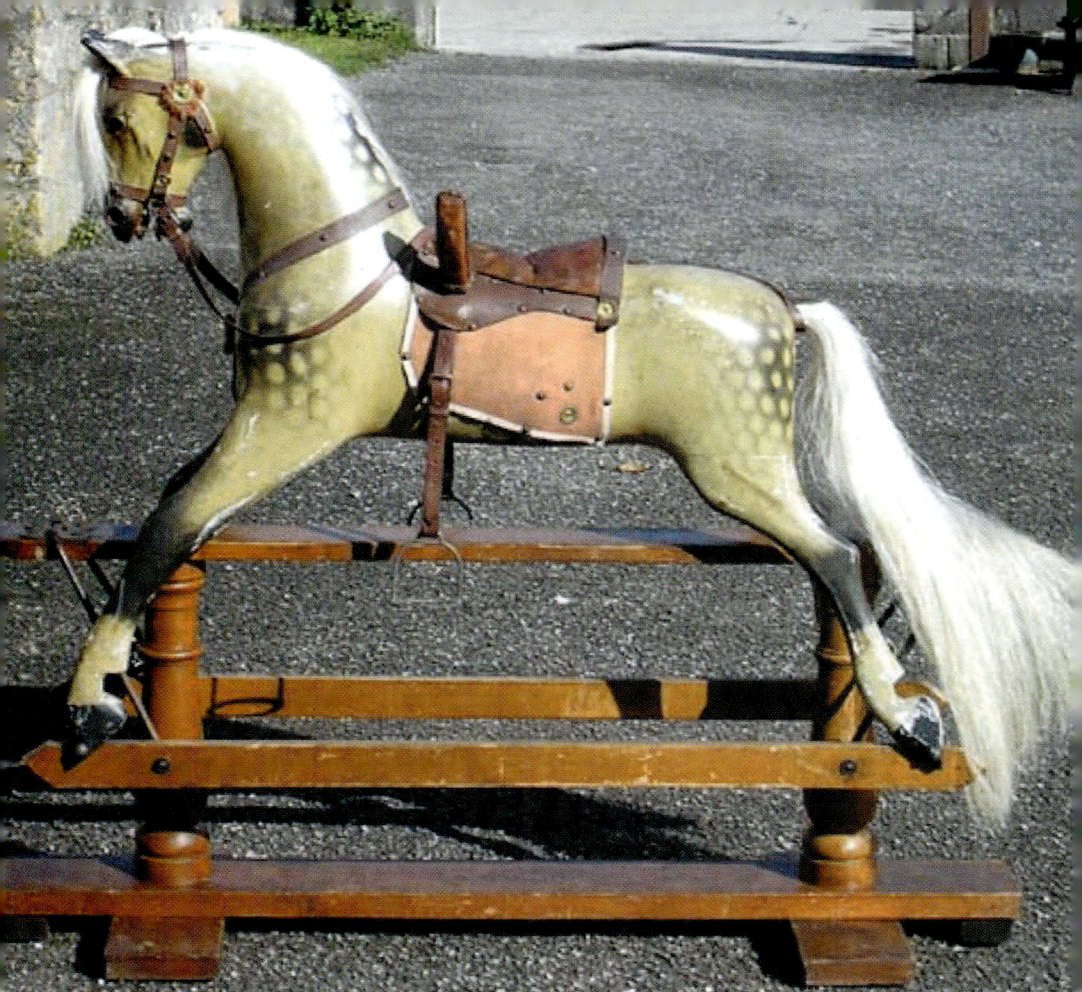

As well as repairing a battered old horse & making it safe for use, a good restorer will be able to faithfully reproduce the particular style of paintwork of the original maker. Where the original paintwork survives, even if it is damaged, it may be better to repair it, rather than re-paint.

The Ayres horse (above), has been given a new mane & tail by Jane Hooker, but the original paintwork has been left as it was. The one on the right will need some fairly extensive restoration work to the dappling, as well as new leatherwork & hair.

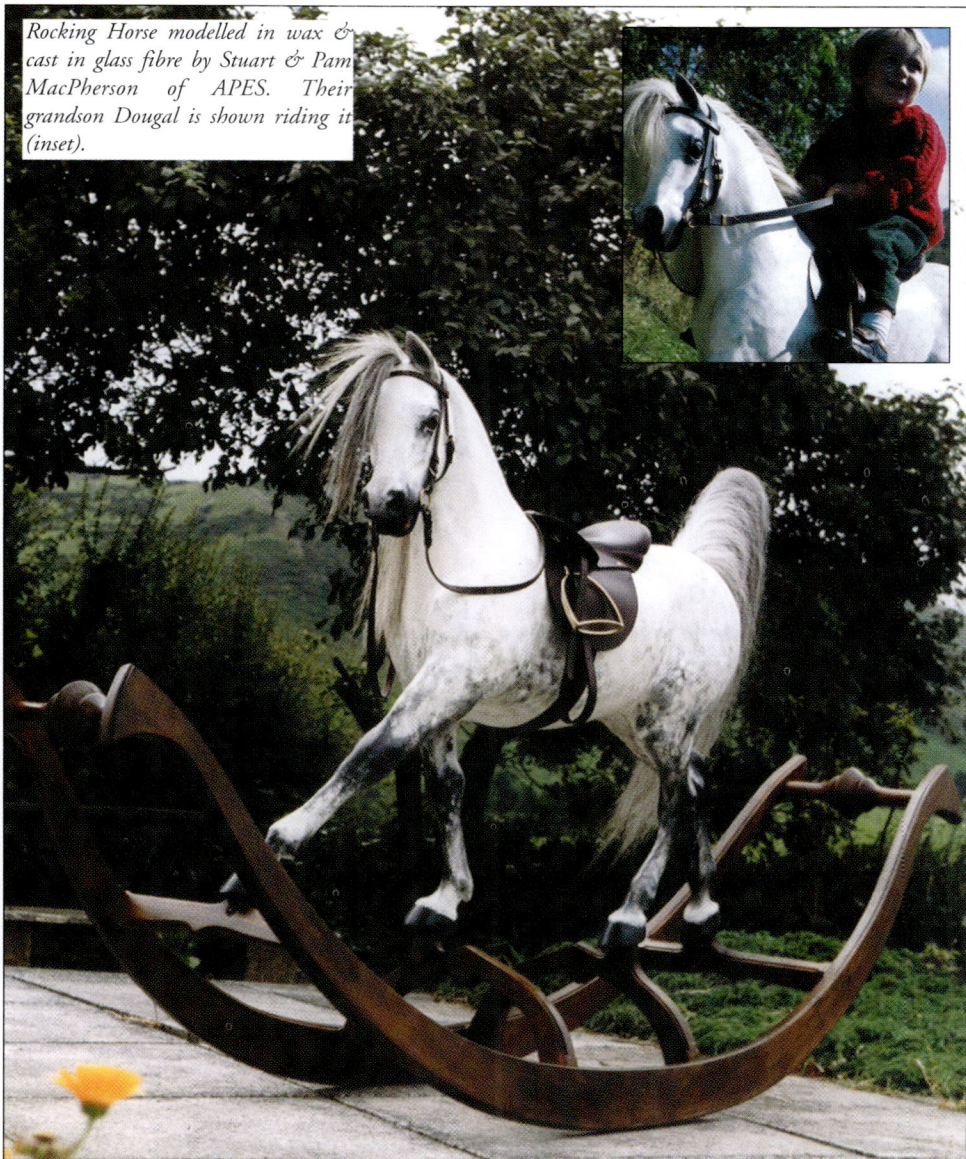

Rocking Horse modelled in wax & cast in glass fibre by Stuart & Pam MacPherson of APES. Their grandson Dougal is shown riding it (inset).

Opposite Page, clockwise from top left - polished hardwood horse by Bernard Woolley; rocking motorbike by Colin & Ann Carlson of Creations in Wood; hobby horses by Lynne Mulcock of Laurel Designs; two of Robert Mullis's horses; horse's head & soft hobby horses by Alan & Jackie Mitchell of Stablemates; rocking horse (with teddy bear) by Nathan Jennings, & Nathan at work - good to see a young man coming into the craft; a pair of heads & horse by Paul Dinan of Handcarved Horses, with his own 'movement locking device'; girl riding a horse made by amateur woodworker Rocklee Bogseth using a design from Anthony Dew's Rocking Horse Shop.

Progress & The Future

"I was shocked by its evil expression. His ferocious upper lip snarled & twisted over huge clipped yellow teeth." Thus Diana Holman Hunt in 1905, on finding her father's old Rocking Horse in the attic. Few makers would wish for such a reaction, but certainly some Victorian Horses with their big teeth can, to a small child looking up, be very intimidating.

Modern makers often strive to give their horses a less aggressive demeanour, & they are safer. Current Toy Safety regulations, coupled with our increasingly litigious society, oblige contemporary makers to give much more attention to the safe use of their Horses than was necessary in earlier times.

One occasionally used to hear horror stories of contaminated materials used as stuffing, eyes that could be pulled out to reveal metal spikes, paints & leathers containing lead & so on. Today such reports are extremely rare. Makers now have access to an array of materials much more suited to their purpose than was available in the past. Paints, leathers & hair are now readily available with all the necessary certifications for compliance with Toy Safety Regulations.

Some people believe that Health & Safety considerations, albeit with worthy intent, have gone too far. An ill-conceived 2003 regulation altering the European Toy Safety Standard would have banned all but the tiniest of Rocking Horses & destroyed the traditional craft.

The news provoked a series of media features & heartfelt protests & lobbying by the British Toymaker's Guild, the Guild of Rocking Horse Makers & others. Eventually the amendment was withdrawn & rocking horse makers breathed a collective sigh of relief.

All makers advocate the high quality of their work. Some are more or less competent than others, but I am convinced that in addition to heightened safety standards, the quality of craftsmanship being produced by the best contemporary makers is higher today than ever. The best Rocking Horses are beautiful works of art & craftsmanship, as well as functioning playthings.

A Rocking Horse is a marvellous plaything, gentle or exciting at the will of the rider, a wonderful vehicle for a child's developing imagination. It is an extremely simple & appealing concept, & the rocking action speaks to a very basic human response. Also, as a project to make, it is fascinating. Both Rocking Horses & the craft that brings them into being are valuable & vital, as much now in the 21st Century as a 100 years ago, if not more so.

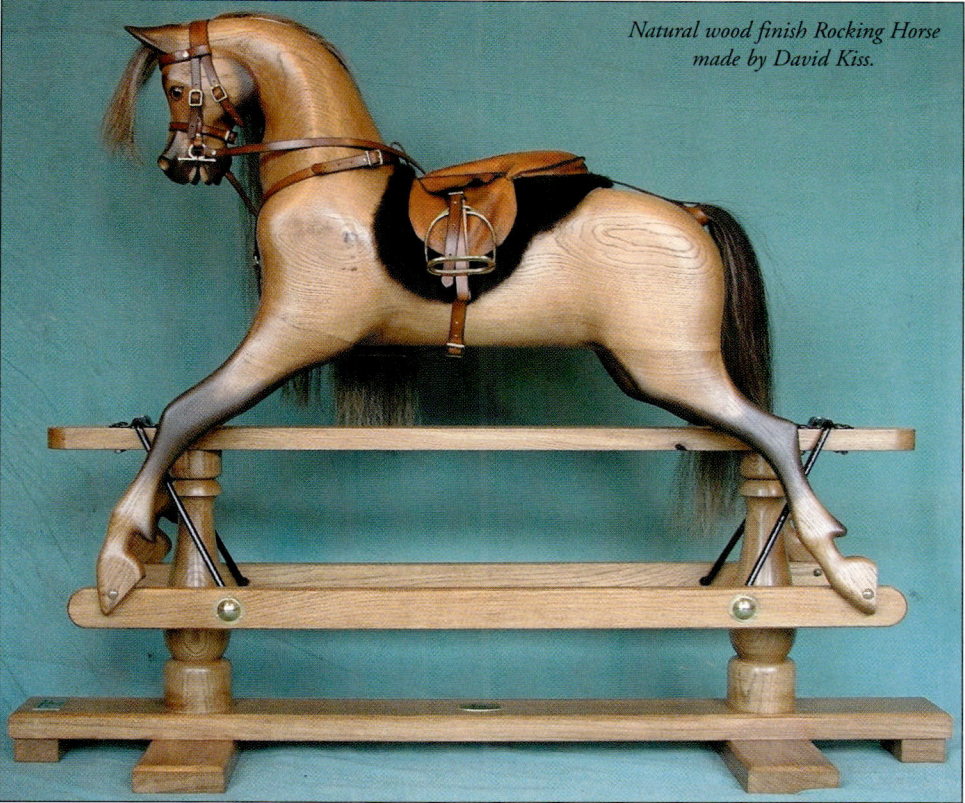

Natural wood finish Rocking Horse made by David Kiss.

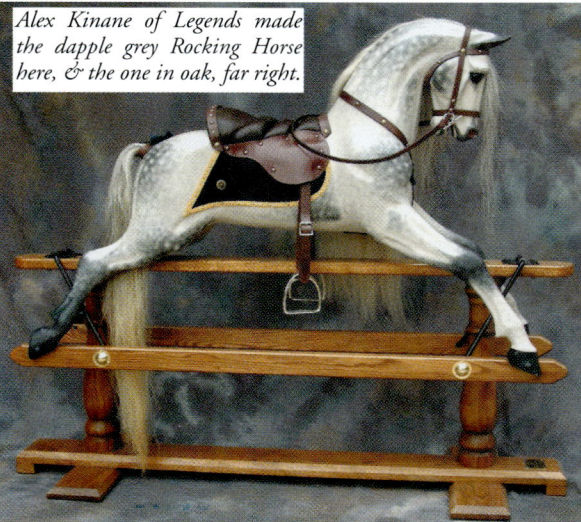

Alex Kinane of Legends made the dapple grey Rocking Horse here, & the one in oak, far right.

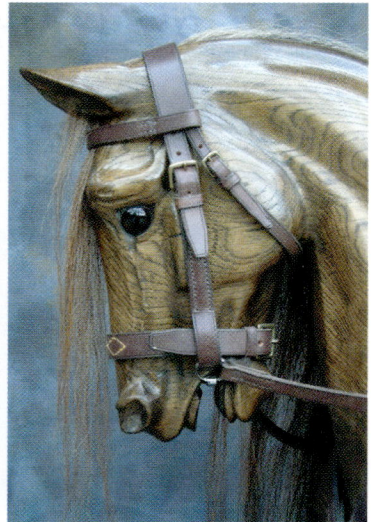

Today the craft is in a relatively healthy position, with many professional makers & restorers in business, & certainly many more amateur enthusiasts than there have ever been. In Britain, perhaps the main concern for professional craftspeople is that increasingly onerous regulation is making it difficult to function.

Also, a major concern for the future of the craft, both professional & amateur, is the decline of school craft as a practical & skill based subject. Lack of basic skills leads to lack of confidence & 'Can do' gives way to 'Can't'.

Making a Rocking Horse is a fascinating & fulfilling challenge. In recent years many amateur woodworkers have overcome their doubts, made a Rocking Horse, & succeeded. Some enjoy the project so much they go on to make rocking horses professionally. Life for the aspiring professional Maker or Restorer is difficult, but many, attracted by the promise of a lifestyle business that can be full, creative & rewarding, are giving it a try, & some of them are succeeding.

Originally made for the Cunard shipping line, this spotted horse was restored by Anthony Dew shown (below) at work on a new Rocking Horse.

(left) Rocking Unicorn made by Legends.

32